THE DAY GO IT RAIN

1 Kings 17—18 FOR CHILDREN

Written brek
Illustr productions

...NG HOUSE, ST. LOUIS, MISSOURI

...TATES OF AMERICA

A wicked man named Ahab
Was king of Israel.
His wife was just as wicked;
Her name was Jezebel.

They worshiped Baal, an idol,
A god they made of wood.
They put him on an altar
And brought him gifts of food.

A servant of Jehovah,
Elijah was his name,
Was sent by God to Ahab
To talk about the rain.

"There's going to be a dry spell
No matter what you do.
Not only will the rain stop,
There won't be any dew."

The king became quite angry
And called Elijah names.
He told his men to seize him
And bind him tight with chains.

Before the men could grab him,
God whisked him far away
Into a place where ravens flew
To bring him food each day.

Next God sent Elijah
To a widow who would give
The little food and drink she had
To help Elijah live.

Elijah found the widow
And asked her for some bread.
She said her food was almost gone
And soon they'd all be dead.

"You need not fear," Elijah said,
"The Lord will care for you.
He will give you flour
And jars of oil too."

The widow baked a loaf of bread,
But just before they ate,
Elijah prayed that God would bless
The food upon their plates.

The widow's son grew sick and died;
Her heart was torn with pain.
Elijah asked the Lord if He
Would give him life again.

The son was soon alive and well.
His mother cried with joy;
She thanked and praised Jehovah
For giving back her boy.

Three years passed by without a drop
Of water from the sky;
The ground was brown and lifeless,
The lakes and rivers dry.

Elijah listened daily
To hear what God would say.
One day God said, "Get ready,
You'll soon be on your way.

"Go and visit Ahab;
Tell him I'll send rain.
All the hills and valleys
Will be fresh and green again."

Elijah went and met
A servant of the king
Who said that Ahab still was mad
And wouldn't hear a thing.

Elijah said, "Tell Ahab
That I am here once more,
And tell him God will send the rain
That we have waited for."

When Ahab saw Elijah,
He said, "See what you've done.
Without the rain to grow things
There's no food for anyone."

"It wasn't I who stopped the rains,"
Elijah told the king.
"The Lord Jehovah rules the earth
And every living thing.

Let's have a test so we will know
The one and only God.
Let's see if Baal can make it rain
On this dry and dusty sod."

"We'll all meet on Mount Carmel
And build two altars there.
Then you can ask your god if he
Has any rain to spare.

"Upon each altar pile some wood
And place a bullock there,
But do not set the wood on fire.
We'll start a fire with prayer."

The morning sun rose bright and clear;
The work was soon begun.
Four hundred fifty prophets worked
Beneath the blazing sun.

They built a altar there to Baal,
An altar made of rocks,
And when it was completed,
They sacrificed an ox.

Elijah worked not far away.
He built an altar too.
He wasn't worried, not a bit.
He knew that God would do.

The prophets prayed that Baal would start
A fire to burn the wood
So they could show Elijah
That their God was very good.

They prayed for half a day or more,
But it was all in vain.
No matter how they screamed and yelled
Their idol sent no rain.

Elijah started teasing.
He said, "I have a hunch
That Baal is either sleeping
Or out somewhere for lunch."

The prophets grew exhausted
And fell upon the ground.
They stopped their noisy wailing;
It was quiet all around.

Elijah stood and raised his arms;
His voice was loud and clear.
The prophets listened as he spoke;
His words reached every ear.

"Pour some water on this wood
And on my offering too,
Then watch the skies and you will see
Just what my God will do."

Then as they watched, Elijah prayed,
"God, let these heathen see
That you alone are Lord of all
For all eternity."

A flash of fire consumed the bull
That lay upon the altar.
It also burned the wood and stones
And dried up all the water.

Soon the air was filled with rain;
It splattered everywhere.
Elijah showed what God will do
When we believe in prayer.

DEAR PARENTS:

The story of Elijah is the forceful and vivid narrative of God's daily intervention in people's lives. It begins with a miraculous drought, continues with the miracles of food and life, and ends with God's miraculous answer to Elijah's prayer, followed by the gift of rain. The story is a very concrete example of the fact that God "richly and daily provides me with all that I need to support this body and life" and more.

The story is also about a magnificent faith. Elijah boldly approaches wicked King Ahab. Elijah believes that God controls life and can raise the dead—literally. Day after day Elijah and the widow depend solely on God for their food. And, to climax the events, Elijah's faith makes him bold enough to challenge 450 false prophets.

It would be well to point out to your child the wonderful relationship between God's providence and our faith. God protects and cares for the faithful; we are faithful and believe God cares for us. The two aspects of the relationship are inseparable.

Let your child talk about his or her daily gifts from God. Then have your child pray, thanking God for specific gifts and asking Him for what is needed. Remember, God does answer prayer, and God gives the faith necessary to pray honestly and fervently.

THE EDITOR